Ancient Greek
Made Simple
Through Stories

CONTENTS

INTRODUCTION

This book was created in conjunction with the Easy Latin Youtube channel found here (where you can find audio lessons):

https://www.youtube.com/c/EasyLatin

The most effective way to learn a language is in context, because not only is it easier to learn new words this way, but you will also acquire grammar organically. And it's much more fun and interesting to learn this way than to memorize grammar tables. In these book, we will be learning directly from simple sentences in Ancient Greek and you may be surprised how easily and quickly you will acquire this beautiful language. Let's go!

LESSON 0

Salvēte omnēs!   Hi everybody!

Before we even start to learn Ancient Greek, we of course need to learn the alphabet. But it's not bad because half of the letters are recognizable. For example, look at this word. Can you read it and figure out its meaning?

βιβλος

It looks like "biblos", right?

You should practice writing down each word by hand as they are presented. This letter λ (lambda) sticks up above the other letters just like a lowercase L, that's how we can remember it. And a bibliography is a list of books, right? This means book. And you can probably guess the next word now that I just said it.

βιβλιογραφια

These letters that look like Bs, though, are pronounced sort of between a B and a V. You put your lips together like when you say B, but say V instead. Let's focus on the end of this word now. First we have this letter γ (gamma), which if you stretch your mind a little, kind of looks like a lower case G without the round part connected. We have to make sure not to confuse it with a Y. And the letter next to it also can be confused with another letter, because this is not a P. This is ϱ (rho), the Greek version of R. This other letter that also kind of looks like a P with a swooping tail is φ (fee) and represents a "ph" sound. It's because of this letter that we have words in

7

English that contain an F sound but are written with PH. This fact will help us learn Greek because most if not all of these words came from Greek, like the following:

φιλοσοφια

This is Philosophy. But wait a second, we already saw an S that looked like this: ς This S is only used at the end of words. When we have an S sound that's not at the end, we use this letter in the middle of φιλοσοφια. This is σ (sigma) and kind of looks like a rolled up S.

π ρ φ

And what was this letter again? γ

It's a G. But it's more of a gargling sound than the English G. Try to read this word now:

δεκα

A decade is how many years? δεκα means "ten". In this word we have a D and a K sound. But notice, "δε" is pronounced just like the English word "they". The letter δ (delta) is a TH sound, not a D sound.

The next word is a little more difficult, but you can probably guess it:

χαρακτηρ

The letter χ (khee) makes a K sound and this other letter that looks like an N is actually the vowel η (eta). This is one of the harder letters to learn, but since it will usually be between two consonants it's not so difficult to remember that this makes a long "ay" sound.

And do you know the letter in the next word?

Αθηναι

This is the city Athens. This letter is θ (theta), which also makes a TH sound.

But note that this is a different TH sound than the one in δ. The TH in θ sound sounds like the TH in "thing" and δ (delta) sounds like the TH in "they". And this word also contains the Greek letter for N, which looks like a V in lower case. This is a good word to write a few times in order to not

8

confuse η (eta) and ν (nu).

And can you guess whose name this is? It was probably the most important name for the Ancient Greeks:

ζευς

This first letter is ζ (zeta) the Greek letter for Z. And the third letter is also easy to mix up. This is υ (upsilon) and it's sound is made by forming the lips in an O shape and saying "ee".

We have to be careful not to confuse this with ν (nu), since these both look like a V, but ν (nu) has a pointed bottom while υ (upsilon) is rounded more like a U.

ν υ

So this first character is an N sound, while the second is like the French "u" sound. And what other letter makes an "eh" sound besides the ε in ζευς?

η

η and ε make the same sound, the only difference is the length. η is the long version of ε.

The next one might be hard to get unless you recognize that this third letter is the symbol for psychology.

ραψωδια

This word is "rhapsody" and the third letter is ψ (psee) and makes a PS sound.

And the other letter next to it that looks like a cross between an O and a W is ω (omega) and makes an O sound. This is the long version of ο (omicron); you can remember that it's longer because it looks like two O's strung together. ο and ε are the only vowels that have a long version.

We have just two letters left. Here's the first:

γαλαξιας

This letter is ξ (ksee) so now can you read this word? Since this makes an X sound, we have to be careful not to confuse this letter with χ (khee), which looks like an X. And the last letter is at the beginning of the next word:

9

μαραθων

This is the name of a city in Greece and now also a race: marathon.

The best way to learn these letters is to write down the words contained in this lesson a few times and just continue reading. But do you see how easy Greek can be? You already knew all the words in this lesson and could practically read them all. Let's try a few more words before we tackle the capital letters.

ευρωπη

This is of course the continent where Greece is located: Europe. And can you guess the meaning of the next word?

καρδια

This means heart, as in cardiac arrest. And what's this word?

χριστιανος

Christian. Remember, the letter that looks like an X makes a "kh" sound, this is why Christmas is sometimes written X-mas. And what did the letter that sounds like an X look like?

ξενοφων

Xenophon is a Greek male name. The X sound is made by this letter that looks like a cursive epsilon. And don't confuse this with epsilon at the beginning of the next word.

επιλογος

Epilogue. And how do we read this next word:

αθλητης

Athlete. Remember, these letters that look like Ns make the same sound as epsilon, only longer. And finally, how do we pronounce this word?

ψυχη

Now let's finish by matching the capital letters to their lower case

counterparts.
These are really easy:

ΑΒΕΖΘΙΚΛΜΝΟΠΤΦΧΨ
α β ε ζ θ ι κ λ μ ν ο π τ φ χ ψ

This leaves us with just a couple difficult ones.

Can you guess what letter this is?

P   This is ϱ

And you might know this one already:

Δ   This is δ

And do you know this one?

Ω   This is ω and kind of looks like an O.

It gets harder from now on. What's this letter?

H   This is η.

We can remember these because they both kind of look like Ns. And this one?

Y   We only have one vowel left, so this is υ.

This one you might not be able to guess.

Γ   This is γ

These next two look somewhat similar, which is which?

Σ   Ξ

The first is σ (ς), which has these two lowercase forms and the second is ξ, which both kind of look like Es, but remember that this makes an X sound. Ok, here's the entire alphabet, and in the next lesson we'll start learning how to speak Ancient Greek!

Α α Β β Γ γ Δ δ Ε ε Ζ ζ
Η η Θ θ Ι ι Κ κ Λ λ Μ μ
Ν ν Ξ ξ Ο ο Π π Ρ ϱ Σ σ/ς
Τ τ Υ υ Φ φ Χ χ Ψ ψ Ω ω

LESSON ONE

Χαίρετε!

Let's start the first lesson of Ancient Greek!

If you already know Latin, some aspects of Greek will come really easily, because several of the forms of declension and conjugation are similar to their Latin counterparts as we'll see very soon. There are also many borrowed words and some words are exactly the same, like the following: there are only three declensions, no ablative form, and two types of regular conjugation for verbs. And the really nice thing is that several of the forms of declension are similar to Latin declension as we'll see very soon. There are also many borrowed words and some words are exactly the same, like the following:

ἐγώ

This is ego, the same as in Latin. To remember this word, imagine that someone with a big ego (ἐγώ) is always thinking about themselves. And just like in Latin, we only use it for emphasis. We don't need to say "I" or "s/he" or "you" etc if it's clear from context..

Ignore the symbols above the vowels for now, but note that the G in Greek is sort of a gargling sound. And don't worry if you haven't studied Latin, I will be making references to help those with Latin knowledge, but also references for those who haven't studied any language.

Let's learn our first sentence in Ancient Greek:

Γράφω.

This means, I write or I draw. An autoGRAPH is your own writing.

And think about it, the first writing was done on clay tablets, so people had to enGRAVE or carve when they were writing. But did you notice something really nice? The first-person ending is the same as in Latin! In Latin we have:

Scrībō.

and in Greek Γράφω. Both words end in a long O, matching the O in ego (ἐγώ). Now the word for book is:

βιβλίον

So what do you think the following word means? (It's a noun.)

Βιβλιογράφος

Literally, book writer. And this word should be obvious.

Βιβλιογραφία

Bibliography Look at the endings of these words now.

Βιβλιογράφος   βιβλίον   Βιβλιογραφία

Do you see a connection to Latin? Which do you think is feminine? Which is neuter? And which is masculine?

The neuter nouns end in ν or N just like the word neuter. And which ending sounds more feminine? ος or α? Lots of feminine names end in A, right? Maria, Jessica. And some names are converted to a feminine form with an A, like Daniela, Brianna, etc.

If you know Latin, then the connection should also be clear, except that instead of the endings "-us" and "-um" for masculine and neuer, we have "-os" and "-on", which look pretty similar to their Latin counterparts. But unlike Latin, Greek has a word for THE, so we have to say:

Τὸ βιβλίον

Can you guess how to say, "I write the book"?

14

Τὸ βιβλίον γράφω.

(Just like in Latin, the accusative and nominative forms of neuter nouns match.)

If you know Latin, using what you know about Scrībō, try to guess how to say, You write.

Γράφεις.

This combination of ε and ι is pronounced with an "ee" sound, just like the "ee" in

Scrībis.

And the third-person form follows the pattern of Latin, but leaves the T off the end. So what is it?

Γράφει.

For those who don't know Latin, look at this chart now.

I	Γράφω
You	Γράφεις
S/he	Γράφει

The "you" and "s/he" forms are the reverse of English in which we add an S to the "s/he" form. We say "you write" and "s/he writes", but it's the reverse in Greek. And as I said earlier, the first-person ends in ω (omega) matching the O in ego (ἐγώ).

For masculine nouns, we have a different word for the:

ὁ βιβλιογράφος

This accent over the omicron is a breath mark, signifying that there is an H sound, so ὁ is pronounced, "ho".

And what was the neuter form of the?

15

τό

So we have τό and ὁ (ho).

Now let's try to say, "The writer writes the book".

Ὁ βιβλιογράφος γράφει τό βιβλίον.
It's practically the same words repeated.

Look at the following sentence now.

Καλῶς γράφει.

What one English word do these two words sound like?

Calligraphy

And what is calligraphy?

Beautiful writing.

The adjective καλός means "good" or "beautiful" and we can form adverbs by replacing ός with ῶς. The longer O sound is like adding -ly to beautiful.

καλός = beautiful → καλῶς = beautifully

Now is a good time to talk about these accent marks. The marks over the vowels here denote differences in pitch. Ancient Greek varied in pitch, so it is thought that it kind of sounded like it was being sung. It's okay to completely ignore these because in fact no one knows exactly how pitch accent worked in Ancient Greek since we obviously have no audio recordings. But it is thought that the difference between these two vowels is in the length and rise in pitch. Nevertheless, you can simply put the emphasis of the word on this syllable, because that is what these accent marks eventually turned into in Koine and Modern Greek.

ός is a short vowel with a small rise in pitch, while

ῶς is longer with a rise and fall in pitch. We'll talk more about this as we go along.

Now, how did we say. "It is a book", in Latin?

Liber est.

Here is the equivalent in Greek:

Βιβλίον ἐστί.

It's just est with ι (iota) at the end. For those who don't know Latin, ἐστί looks a lot like "is", doesn't it? That's because these words came from the same Indo-European word that sounded something like "hésti".

And in Ancient Greek we don't need to say anything for "a". We just say, "Book is."

Note that this accent above the ἐ (epsilon) is different from the two we just saw and the one we saw over the omicron in:

ὁ

These are known as breath marks.

The one over the omicron signifies an H sound and the one over the epsilon signifies that it doesn't make an H sound. It's really annoying, because they could have just put no mark, but it's just one of those things that we have to get used to.

Before we look at the next word, try to recall the name for a doctor who treats children...A pediatrician. So what do you think this means:

Παιδίον ἐστί.

It is a (little) child.

Now, to say "you are" in Latin, we remove the T from est. But in Greek we remove both the Tau and sigma and are left with the following word:

Παιδίον εἶ.

You are a child. Now we have a breath mark and a pitch accent mark. So what do these two marks mean...? They signify that the pitch of the word rises and falls and that there is no H sound.

Congratulations on speaking your first sentences in Ancient Greek! See you in the next lesson!

LESSON 2

Χαίρετε!

Welcome to the second lesson of Ancient Greek!

We'll be reviewing the words we learned in the first lesson, so if you're a little shaky, you might want to review that lesson first. But by the end of this lesson we will be able to read our first quote in Greek! Let's start with saying, I write the book.

Τὸ βιβλίον γράφω.

We're going to change this now to say, "I have the book."

Τὸ βιβλίον ἔχω.

"I have" is, ἔχω. Don't confuse this with ἐγώ.

And note that the accent is on the opposite syllable in each word. It might help to connect ἔχω to the word annex, "to add to". Like "annἔχω". To make something HOLD or HAVE something. But we will also repeat this word a lot, so it should be pretty easy to learn.

Try to say now, "You have a child."

Παιδίον ἔχεις.

Remember, a doctor for children is a pediatrician, so "child" is παιδίον in Greek.

And the conjugation we have learned so far is similar to Latin conjugation. Let's say now, "The writer writes beautifully."

Ὁ βιβλιογράφος καλῶς γράφει.

Remember, καλῶς is the adverb form of καλός which means "beautiful" or "good". (We learned that καλῶς γράφει sounds like calligraphy.)

Let's move on to some new words now. Try to guess how to say mathematician in Greek. It's a masculine noun:

ὁ μαθηματικός

A+ if you remembered the ὁ. ;)

And since one could argue that all of knowledge stems from mathematics, a student is a:

μαθητής

Try to say now, "You are the student." Can you remember the word for "you are"?

Εἶ ὁ μαθητής.

The next sentence is related, but sort of the opposite. Can you figure it out?

Εἰμί ὁ διδάσκαλος.

I am the teacher.

An autoDIDACT is someone who teaches themselves. Additionally, something "didactic" is something instructive. And instead of "sum", Greek has the word εἰμι, which conveniently contains the word "me". Let's say now, "I am", "you are", and "he/she/it is".

εἰμί   εἶ   ἐστί

They seem more related than the words for "to be" in Latin and English.

Let's repeat the words for teacher and student since they were a little complicated.

μαθητής   and   διδάσκαλος

Or completely in Greek:

μαθητής καὶ διδάσκαλος.

And do you see how the accent over καὶ goes in the other direction?

This is the last of the accents and indicates a more acute rise in pitch than the accents over the other two words. But, again, this is just supposition, because we don't really know exactly what Ancient Greek sounded like.

The next sentence will help you remember how to say teacher.

Καλῶς διδάσκεις.

You teach well. Or you teach beautifully.

Did you notice that διδάσκαλος contains the word καλος? If we remove most of this, then we have the stem form of the verb (διδάσκ-). And here's how we negate a verb:

Οὐ διδάσκει.

It does not teach. Or more poetically, "does not make one wise".

This will be in the quote, so take note of it. Another word we will need is:

Πολλὰ βιβλία ἔχει.

First, if you studied Latin, what do you think that βιβλία means?

It's the plural form βιβλίον. Neutral nouns in Ancient Greek follow the same pattern as Latin. The nominative and accusative plural both end in "-α".

If you don't know what any of this means, don't worry. You just need to know that Ancient Greek doesn't just add an S like in English: the end of the word changes to form the plural. So βιβλίον (book) becomes βιβλία (books). It's similar to how "woman" changes to "women" in plural, except that this happens with all nouns in Ancient Greek, not just the irregular nouns.

And now can you guess what Πολλὰ means? You have probably heard the words "polygamy" and "polytheistic" and can figure out that this sentence means, "S/he has many books".

Now, can you guess what the following word means?

πολυμαθής
Note that the end of the word is not μαθητής.

This means literally "much learning". A polymath is someone who has broad knowledge, usually of many fields of science and art, like Da Vinci and Benjamin Franklin. But before we dissect the quote, try to figure out what these words mean:

πρῶτον μάθημα

What's a PROTOtype? It's the first model.

So this is a "first learning".......in other words, the first lesson. And for the quote, we will see the word

νόον

which is contained in the word "paranoia" and means "mind". Paranoid literally means, "beyond" + "mind" + "medical condition". So what does this mean?

Πολυμαθῆ νόον ἔχειν οὐ διδάσκει.

Being learned does not make one wise. Some words like ἔχει add a "ν" at the end when they are at the end of the sentence or when the next word begins with a vowel, like the word "a" in English which becomes "an" according to the same rule.

22

So literally this means:

"having a knowledgable mind does not teach"

Okay, in the next lesson we'll tackle some more wise quotes from the Greeks that involve many of these words, so see you then!

LESSON 3

Χαίρετε!

We learned a lot of new words in the last lesson, so let's use them some more. How do we say student?

μαθητής

And there was a related word we learned that means lesson. Do you remember how to say, "first lesson"?

πρῶτον μάθημα

Remember, a prototype is a first model.

This -μα (ma) ending carried over into Latin, like the following words:

systēma
problēma
thema
clima

and makes verbs into neuter third-declension nouns.

The word γράφω is made into

24

γράμμα

and what do we write? A letter. (As in from the alphabet.) So let's say, "You write a letter."

Γράμμα γράφεις.

Remember, neuter nouns are the same in nominative and accusative form just like in Latin. And now, what do you think this means?

Γράμματα μανθάνει.

He or she learns letters. The "τα" ending makes these types of nouns plural and also is the plural version of "the". So for "the letters", we have

τὰ γράμματα

And since this is a neuter noun, how would we say "the letter"?

τὸ γράμμα

The form of "the" only changes for gender, not declension. Let's look at these μαθ ("math") words a little closer.

μαθητής	μάθημα	μανθάνω
student	lesson	I learn

The last one is a little different and contains two ν's, but the connection should be clear. Let's try to say now, "The student learns the lesson."

Ὁ μαθητὴς μανθάνει τὸ μάθημα.

We already learned the word for first lesson, so what do you think this means?

Δεύτερον καὶ τρίτον μάθημα.

Second and third lesson. The word Deuteronomy was derived from δεύτερος even though it's the fifth book of the Bible. And do you know the Greek word for two? It's in several English words as well as a famous language learning app.

25

δύο

And the word for "three" is not difficult either, it's:

τρεῖς

Here's another free word:

Τὸ βιβλίον μικρὸν ἔχει.

The meaning of μικρός should be pretty obvious, since it's in the word MICROscopic. But notice that the end of the word changes to match βιβλίον, which is a neuter noun. μικρός is the masculine version. The meaning of this sentence is: S/he has the small book. And can you guess the meaning of the next sentence?

Ὁ κόσμος μέγας ἐστίν.

The universe is big. Or the cosmos is big. So "big" and "small" are?

μέγας καὶ μικρός

Pretty easy, right? Mega and micro. So how do we say, "The child is small"?

Τὸ παιδίον μικρὸν ἐστίν.

And finally, how do we say, "You have many books"?

Πολλὰ βιβλία ἔχεις.

The plural marker of neuter nouns is "-a", (just like in Latin) and πολύς is found in the words polygamy and polytheistic. Let's learn the first half of today's quote now:

Γράμματα μανθάνειν δεῖ

I like to think of this word δεῖ as meaning, "there is debt", since it looks a little like debt and means, "there is need of". It is an impersonal verb, so a good translation of this phrase would be: One must learn letters. And

26

μανθάνειν is the infinitive, or dictionary form, of μανθάνω. Like saying, "to learn". The second half is a little harder, we have:

καὶ μανθόντα νόον ἔχειν.

So altogether it's:

Γράμματα μανθάνειν δεῖ καὶ μανθόντα νόον ἔχειν.

One must learn letters, and learning them have reason.

Ok, we'll go through more wise quotes from the Greeks in the next lesson! See you then!

LESSON 4

Χαίρετε!

We're going to learn a few words that are useful for reading the New Testament of the Bible and also go through a few passages from it.

But before we continue I need to explain a really difficult part of Ancient Greek that I have been glossing over until now.

Sometimes in order to learn a foreign language, it's helpful to notice a few things about our native language first. Think about the sentence, "She hugs him". "She" is the subject, because it is the noun that the verb matches in form. If the subject were "I", then the verb would change to "hug". But since it's "she", we add an "-s" to the verb. The subject is the noun that does the verb.

And "him" is the object. It is the noun the action is being done TO. But notice: we don't say, "She hugs he". "He" changes its form to "him" when it's the object. And in Ancient Greek, it's not just the pronouns like "he" that change, but all nouns change like this. So in Ancient Greek, instead of just "She hugs the dog", we would say something like, "She hugs the dogem". Because the noun changes when it's the object, just like "he" changes to "him" and "she" changes to "her". We saw this form change already with the plural versions of nouns, in which βιβλίον (book) changed to βιβλία (books).

But just like in English, there are more forms than just "him" and "her", we also have "his". As in "his book". So in Ancient Greek there is a possessive form for each noun, similar to how in English we add an apostrophe S, as in "the dog's ball". However, there are other forms in Ancient Greek that English does not use that we'll be exploring in this book.

Let's explore how the subject form changes when it becomes the object form, just like how "he" changes to "him" when it's the object in English. We will use the following masculine noun:

ἄγγελος

When there are two γ's, they make an NG sound, so this is pronounced "angelos" with a hard G (like the word "angle", not "angel"). Do you know what this means?

Angel, or messenger.

And what were the Apostles? They were the Twelve Disciples that Jesus SENT to spread the Gospel. So can you figure out this sentence?

Ἀποστέλλω τὸν ἄγγελον.

I send the messenger. The subject is ἐγώ although it is left unstated and the object is ἄγγελος, but look at the ending of ἄγγελος in the sentence above: it ends in "-ν" in order to indicate that it is the object. Likewise, ὁ gets changed to τὸν. This is because ἄγγελος is what I am sending, so we have to change it's form, because in Ancient Greek word order is flexible. If we changed the sentence to "S/he sends the messenger":

Ἀποστέλλει τὸν ἄγγελον.

we would only know that ἄγγελος is the object because of the change in the ending. If words didn't change their endings, we might confuse the subject and object in sentences like these.

However, neuter nouns don't change their form. Do you remember how to say, "He writes the letter"? (As in letter from the alphabet.)

Τὸ γράμμα γράφει.

And how about, "I have the small book"?

Τὸ βιβλίον μικρόν ἔχω.

Since these are both neuter nouns, the subject and object forms are the same. Even the word for "the" remains he same: τὸ. But this doesn't happen for masculine or feminine nouns.

And now here is a passage from the Bible in Greek. This is Matthew 11:10:

Ἀποστέλλω τὸν ἄγγελον μου.

I send my messenger.
When we want to say "my (something)," we sandwich the "something" between the word for "the" and μου. Remember this, because we will see it again in a moment.

If theology is the study of god, how do you think we would say "the god" in Ancient Greek.

ὁ θεὸς

The next word might be difficult unless you've read lots of Plato.

ὁ λόγος

Is found in the word "diaLOGue", and means "the word".

Can you guess what passage this is? This is the first line of the Gospel of John:

Θεὸς ἦν ὁ λόγος.

The word was God. John 1:1

The word ἦν is past tense, which we're not going to deal with right now, so let's change this to the present tense. How would we say, "The word is God"?

Θεὸς ἐστί ὁ λόγος.

Something to note is that in this sentence, θεὸς is not preceded by ὁ, this is because the ὁ marks the subject. In Ancient Greek, like Latin, word order does not change the meaning of the sentence, so although θεὸς comes first, the ὁ in front of λόγος tells us that this sentence means, "The word is God." and not "God is the word."

See you in the next lesson!

LESSON 5

Χαίρετε!

In this lesson we're going to start introducing something called declensions. But we'll be using some easy words to begin with. Here is how to say, "the Italy":

ἡ Ἰταλία

What gender is this? Feminine, because it ends with α. This is known as a noun of the first declension, which just means that nouns of this type follow the same declension pattern. For example, we already saw that ἄγγελος becomes ἄγγελον when it is the object. This is a second declension noun and all nouns of this type change to -ον when they are the object.

That's all that declensions are: the pattern that the nouns follow when they change forms. Here is the declension of "he" and "I":

I   me   my
he   him   his

You see, "I" and "he" are the form we use for the subject, which we will start calling the **"nominative** form". "Me" and "him" are the form we use for the object (as in "she hit him"), which we will start calling the **"accusative** form". And "my" and "his" are the possessive form (as in "my book"), which we will start calling the **"genitive** form".

So we have already learned that ἄγγελος is the nominative form and that changing the -ος ending to -ον changes the word to the accusative form

32

(ἄγγελον). And you may be realizing now that the neuter nouns we have been using up to now don't change: βιβλίον and παιδίον have the same nominative and accusative forms.

We will be learning the different forms for Ancient Greek nouns as we go along, but because this is one of the most difficult parts of the language, we will be taking it slow.

But there are two different types of feminine first-declension nouns, because the following is another one:

ἡ Εὐρώπη

First-declension feminine nouns in Ancient Greek all end in either η or α, but the α can be either short or long. And there are also masculine first-declension nouns, but these all end in either -ης or -ᾱς, where the α is long. Now something a little infuriating is that the following noun is third-declension and feminine, because it has a short α:

ἡ Ἑλλάς

Do you know what this means?

"the Greece"

You may have heard of *Hellenic* literature or heard the word *Hellene*, referring to the Ancient Greeks. Now you know where this word came from. But notice, the word for "the" only depends on the gender of the noun, not the declension, which makes things much easier. Adjectives function the same way. Can you remember the word for beautiful?

καλός

Here is how we say, Greece is beautiful.

Ἡ Ἑλλὰς καλή.

The endings of adjectives almost always match the word for "the". Do you remember the three words for "the" that we've learned? List the masculine, feminine, and neuter versions.

ὁ ἡ τό

Can you guess what the following sentence means?

Ἡ Ἰταλία ἐν τῇ Εὐρώπῃ ἐστίν.

Italy is in Europe. (ῃ is pronounced "ey-ee")

Here in the words τῇ Εὐρώπῃ we have a new form called the dative case. This form has several uses, but for now we'll focus on one: the word following ἐν is always in the dative form when talking about location.

So it's:

ἐν τῇ Εὐρώπῃ

We change ἡ to τῇ in the dative case. And Εὐρώπη changes to Εὐρώπῃ.

(And for Latin speakers, do you remember what the dative case of Eurōpa was in Latin?

Eurōpae. It's very similar, right? Especially for the nouns that end in α.)

So can you guess what the dative of ἡ Ἰταλία is?

τῇ Ἰταλίᾳ

(Which is very similar to Ītaliae in Latin, right?)

If you remember back, we saw once how to neglect a statement. Do you remember how to say "not"?

οὐ

(It is pronounced "oo")

But when the next word begins with a vowel, it changes to:

34

οὐκ

So how do we say, "it is not"?

οὐκ ἐστί

In Ancient Greek, the word Asia is:

Ἀσία

Let's try to say now, "Greece is not in Asia."

Ἡ Ἑλλὰς οὐκ ἐστίν ἐν τῇ Ἀσίᾳ.

Now, the word for "I see" is

ὁρῶ

This kind of sounds like "aware", if that helps.

You might also see this written as ὁράω, but we are going to use ὁρῶ since this is more common in Ancient Greek literature. So try to say now, "I see the book".

Τὸ βιβλίον ὁρῶ.

Remember, this is accusative form even though it looks the same as the nominative. And here is how to say, "I see Italy".

Τὴν Ἰταλίαν ὁρῶ.

Do you see the pattern? It ends with -ν just like second-declension nouns.

And I bet you can now guess how to say, "I see Europe".

Τὴν Εὐρώπην ὁρῶ.

And finally, how would we say, "I see the angel"?

Τὸν ἄγγελον ὁρῶ.

The first and second-declensions are kind and all end in ν in the accusative form (just like how the Latin accusative form always ends in M). We'll continue exploring the declensions in the next lessons.

LESSON 6

Χαίρετε!

In the last lesson we learned how to say, "I see." Do you remember what it was?

ὁρῶ

And a few lessons ago we learned the word for student. Let's say, "the student."

ὁ μαθητής

What declension and gender is this?

It's a first-declension masculine noun. What were the two masculine endings?

-ης and -ᾱς with a long α.

We're going to say now, "You see the student."

Τὸν μαθητὴν ὁρᾷς.

Remember how I said in the last lesson that ὁρῶ is sometimes written as ὁράω? This is because ὁρῶ is the contracted form of ὁράω. So while the "you" form of ὁράω is ὁράεις, as we'd expect, the ει sound in the "you" form of ὁρῶ gets contracted to ὁρᾷς. It becomes that little ι below the α.

And how did we say, "The student learns"?

Ὁ μαθητὴς μανθάνει.

It is almost the same as student, but slips a ν in at the beginning.

And we also learned another related word and a longer sentence. Let's try to say now, "The student learns the lesson."

Ὁ μαθητὴς μανθάνει τὸ μάθημα.

We also learned two other related words. Do you remember how to say, "You write a letter"?

Γράμμα γράφεις.

And can you guess what the following word means?

Ἱπποπόταμος

Hippopotamus. Obviously English adopted this word from Greek, although through Latin, which is why the ending changed. Let's try to say now, "I have a small hippopotamus."

Τὸν ἱπποπόταμον μικρὸν ἔχω.

Now the reason we learned this word is not just because it's a "gimme", but because it is composed of two other words: Ἱπποπόταμος literally means, "river horse." Horse is ἵππος and river is ποταμός.

Let's say now, "He or she sees the river."

Τὸν ποταμὸν ὁρᾷ.

Remember, to get the third-person conjugation of most verbs, we just remove the final ς from the "you" form. And can you figure out the next sentence?

Ὁ Νεῖλος ἐστί ποταμός.

The Nile is a river.

And now can you guess what this word means?

ἡ πόλις

It's in the word metroPOLIS and means, "the city".

"The Sparta" in Ancient Greek is pronounced:

ἡ Σπάρτη

Let's try to say now, "Sparta is a city."

Ἡ Σπάρτη ἐστί πόλις.

And do you remember how to say, "The Greece" from the last lesson?

ἡ Ἑλλάς

The dative form is a little unpredictable since this is a third-declension noun. It's:

τῇ Ἑλλάδι

Let's try to say now, "Sparta is in Greece."

Ἡ Σπάρτη ἐν τῇ Ἑλλάδι ἐστίν.

Now the way to say "what" in Greek is

τίς

if referring to something masculine or feminine and simply

τί

if referring to something neuter or nondescript.

And what Latin word is this similar to?

quis

This next sentence might blow your mind:

Τί ἐστίν ἡ Ῥώμη;

"What is Rome?" In Greece, the semicolon is used to indicate a question, which takes a little getting used to.

Ok, let's answer this question now.

Ἡ Ῥώμη ἐστί μεγάλη πόλις.

Rome is a big city.

If you remember, the masculine version of this adjective was μέγας but it's a little irregular and often uses the stem: μεγάλ- which is in the words "megalomania" and "acromegaly".

And finally, here's the neuter form of this adjective:

Βιβλίον μέγα ἔχω.

I have a big book.

Ok, in the next lesson we'll start reading our first story in Greek, so stay tuned!

LESSON 7

Χαίρετε!

Let's review some of the harder things we learned. Do you remember how to say "The Greece"?

ἡ Ἑλλάς

And what was the dative form?

τῇ Ἑλλάδι

So let's use this in the phrase, "Sparta is in Greece."

Ἡ Σπάρτη ἐν τῇ Ἑλλάδι ἐστίν.

In Ancient Greek, the word for "I live" as in I inhabit, or reside, is:

οἰκέω

which comes from the word οἶκος, meaning "house". And you may have heard of towns in England that end in -wick or -wich, like Warwick and Southwick. The word "vicinity" also has connections to these words.

But οἰκέω often gets contracted to

οἰκῶ

which we will be using. Do you remember the other contracted word we learned?

ὁρῶ

meaning, "to see". These look a little similar, so we have to be careful not to mix them up.

And how do we say, "I see the river"?

Τὸν ποταμὸν ὁρῶ.

Remember, hippopotamus means, "river horse", which is how we learned the word for river. And let's try to say now, "I live in Greece."

Ἐν τῇ Ἑλλάδι οἰκῶ.

And can you understand this phrase?

Τὸ ὄνομα μοι Ἡρακλῆς ἐστιν.

My name is Hercules. Remember, the capital H isn't an H in Greek, it's the letter η (eta). It's the little mark in front of this letter that makes an "h" sound. (The word ὄνομα looks somewhat similar to the Latin: nōmen.) And can you guess what gender ὄνομα is? Remember, almost all words ending in -μα are neuter.

So let's try to say, "My name is beautiful".

Τὸ ὄνομα μοι καλόν ἐστιν.

We're going to learn one more word before we begin the story:

γεωργός

It's like the Greek version of George, but this means farmer. It is composed of three parts:

γῆ ("earth") + ἔργον ("work") + -ος

the first is γῆ, which means "earth", like in γεωγραφία, the study of the physical properties of the earth; the second is ἔργον, which is in the word synergy, working together. So this is literally a "worker of the earth", hence farmer; and then we have the suffix -ος, which makes it a masculine second declension noun.

Okay, we're ready now to tackle the beginning of this story.

ἐγὼ εἰμὶ παιδίον Ἑλληνικόν, οἰκῶ ἐν ἀγροῖς· ἐν τοῖς ἀγροῖς γεωργός ἐστιν, ὃς γεωργεῖ καὶ ἔχει οἶκον·

Could you figure out the beginning?

"I am a Greek child."

Ἑλληνικός is the adjective form of Ἕλλην, the noun form. In English these are the same word: Greek. Then we have:

οἰκῶ ἐν ἀγροῖς.

What do we know about ἐν? That the following word will be in dative.

But what would the dative form of ἀγρός be?

τῷ ἀγρῷ

So you might be able to guess that ἀγροῖς is the plural form of ἀγρῷ.

This first sentence then is, "I am a Greek child, I live in the countryside." And in the next sentence we can see the dative plural form of "the". So what does this first part mean? "In the countryside there is a farmer." And can you remember all the masculine versions of "the" that we've learned so far? Let's go through the Nominative, Accusative, and Dative.

43

ὁ   τὸν   τῷ

Okay, let's finish the story now. What does the word γεωργεῖ look like? A verb in third-person, right? So this means "farms". And can you guess now what ὅς means? We have, "There is a farmer, ____ farms." So this last part means "who farms and has a..." what?

Οἶκος means house. So how would we say, "The farmer lives in the house"?

Γεωργός ἐν τῷ οἴκῳ οἰκεῖ.

Okay, here is the story one more time, with its English translation:

ἐγὼ εἰμὶ παιδίον Ἑλληνικόν, οἰκῶ ἐν ἀγροῖς· ἐν τοῖς ἀγροῖς γεωργός ἐστιν, ὃς γεωργεῖ καὶ ἔχει οἶκον·

I am a Greek child, living in the countryside; in the countryside there is a farmer who farms and has a house;

We'll continue with this story in the coming lessons, so stick around!

LESSON 8

Χαίρετε!

Let's review. How did we say, "I live"?

οἰκῶ

And can you remember, "I live in Greece"?

Ἐν τῇ Ἑλλάδι οἰκῶ.

What was, "name"?

ὄνομα

And how did we make this into "my name"?

τὸ ὄνομα μοι

Let's say now, "My name is Alexandros."

Τὸ ὄνομα μοι Ἀλέξανδρος ἐστιν.

This will be a name in the story that we're going to have to decline. And in this lesson's part of the story, we will start to learn the Genitive, or possessive form. But Latin won't help us here, because the Genitive form for these second declension masculine nouns that end in -ος is:

τοῦ Ἀλεξάνδρου

So let's say now, "Child of Alexandros" or "Alexandros's child":

παιδίον τοῦ Ἀλεξάνδρου

But there's a different word for child that we'll learn today:

τέκνον

This word is used for one's offspring.

There are some related English words, but they are very obscure. It's best to think, "τέκνον listen to techno music" or something like that, haha. Using this word now, let's say, "I am the child of Alexandros."

τέκνον εἰμι τοῦ Ἀλεξάνδρου.

Let's take a moment now to look at the words for "the" that we've learned so far, because we've now learned all the masculine and neuter versions, because these are the same for all cases except the nominative and accusative, since the neuter forms match in these two cases.

Nom.	ὁ	τό	ἡ
Acc.	τόν	τό	τήν
Gen.	τοῦ	τοῦ	τῆς
Dat.	τῷ	τῷ	τῇ

It's too bad that the neuter nominative and accusative aren't τόν, since they would then match the endings of the nouns, but that's the way non-constructed languages are. But this isn't too difficult to memorize because there is a clear pattern. The masculine and neuter articles all have o and the feminine articles all have ἡ. The accusative generally ends in ν, similar to the M in Latin. The dative cases all just have a long vowel followed by ι. And the genitive is the one we'll simply have to memorize. But it's not too difficult and these will help us with the noun endings.

Let's return to the story now. Another word we have to learn is:

46

ἀδελφός

The word δελφύς means womb, so ἀδελφός means, "same womb". And those who come out of the same womb are brothers and sisters, right?

Maybe you can also associate this word with the Oracle of Delphi, where many Greek heroes went and found out some terrible fate involving their family, like that they would marry their mother and kill their father. So let's say now, "I have a brother."

Ἀδελφὸν ἔχω.

And can you guess how to say, "You have a sister"? We just have to change one vowel.

Ἀδελφήν ἔχεις.

Now, if you remember that for "I am" and "S/he is", we had:

εἰμί ἐστὶν

Well, the version for "We are" is sort of a combination of these, it's:

ἐσμέν

So can you understand this phrase?

Βαρβαροι οὐκ ἐσμὲν.

We are not barbarians.

And can you think of how to say "We are children" using the new word we learned? How do we make it plural?

Ἐσμὲν τέκνα.

We're ready now for the continuation of the story, but there's one word that you will have to guess in the last sentence, so watch out for that.

τέκνον εἰμι τοῦ Ἀλεξάνδρου. καὶ ἔχω ἀδελφόν καὶ ἀδελφήν· τὸ ὄνομα μοι Λεωνίδας ἐστιν. ἐσμὲν οὖν τέκνα τοῦ Ἀλεξάνδρου.

Could you figure out what οὖν means? It means "therefore" or "then", which it kind of sounds like. So here's an English translation of the story:

I am a child of Alexander. And I have a brother and a sister; my name is Leonidas. We are then the children of Alexander.

Okay, we'll continue reading more Ancient Greek in the next lesson! See you then!

LESSON 9

Χαίρετε!

Let's review the versions of "to be" that we've learned so far. How do we say, "I am" and "S/he is"?

εἰμί ἐστί/ἐστίν

Remember, we add a ν if it comes at the end of a sentence or in front of a vowel. And how do we say, "We are"?

ἐσμὲν

It's sort of a combination of the first two. And we learned one more that was shorter. How do we say, "You are"?

εἶ

And do you remember how to say, "I live"?

οἰκῶ

And I mentioned once briefly that this is related to the word "house", which is:

οἶκος

But, we are going to use a different word in this story, which is:

οἰκία

You will see both versions in literature, but the difference is that οἶκος refers to all the property of a person, while οἰκία is specifically the house on that property. And do you know how we change this into dative form to say, "In a house"?

ἐν οἰκίᾳ

So let's try to say, "I live in a house."

Ἐν οἰκίᾳ οἰκῶ.

And do you remember how to say, "the brother"?

ὁ ἀδελφός

And sister was very similar. We just have to change one vowel. Let's say now, "I have a sister."

Ἀδελφήν ἔχω.

Now, looking at ἐσμὲν, how do you think we would change ἔχω to mean, "We have"?

ἔχομεν

And do you remember the word we learned for child in the last lesson?

τέκνον

This is what we use for our offspring. And remember, it's a neuter noun. So let's say, "We have children."

Τέκνα ἔχομεν.

Remember, neuter nouns have the same nominative and accusative forms.

Another word we'll need for the story is:

ἰχθύς

This means fish and is in the words ichthyology, which is the study of fish, and ichthyosaurus, which was the dinosaur that lived in the sea and looks like a scary dolphin. And there's a connection to the Christian fish symbol, which is included in the appendix. And as you may be able to guess, since this word ends differently than every noun we've seen, this is another declension: a third declension noun.

And can you remember how to say, "I see"?

ὁρῶ

Now, fish is a masculine now, so let's try to say, "I see the fish."

Τὸν ἰχθὺν ὁρῶ.

And do you know how to say, "Big fish"?

μέγας ἰχθύς

It's like, "Mega fish". And the final word we need to learn is:

ἐγγύς

I'm not sure if these words are related, but ἐγγύς sounds like "anguish" and Schopenhauer's Hedgehog's dilemma says basically that being near people gives you anguish. This is an adverb, so all we have to do is add it to a sentence. Can you guess what this means?

ἦν ἡ Βηθανία ἐγγὺς τῶν Ἱεροσολύμων.

This is from John 11:18. Bethany was near Jerusalem.

We saw this first word ἦν briefly before; it's just the past tense of ἐστίν, so don't worry about it for now. Ok, we're now ready to read the story.

Ἔχομεν οἰκίαν. Ἡ οἰκία καλή ἐστιν. Ἐγγύς ἐστι ποταμός. Ἰχθύς ἐν τῷ ποτᾶμῷ ἐστίν. Τὸν ἰχθὺν ὁρῶ. Ὁ ἰχθὺς μέγας ἐστίν.

You should be able to understand this by now, but if you need help, here's the English version:

We have a house. The house is beautiful. There is a river nearby. There is a fish in the river. I see the fish. The fish is big.

LESSON 10

What was the new word for house that we learned?

οἰκία

The old word was οἶκος. Remember, οἶκος refers to all the property of a person, while οἰκία is specifically the house on that property. And how did we say, "I live in a house."

Ἐν οἰκίᾳ οἰκῶ.

Do you know what Philadelphia is referred to as? The city of...Brotherly love. And how do we say "brother"?

ἀδελφός

So the rest of Philadelphia must mean "love" and indeed, the word

φίλος

means "that which is loved". Which can be used to mean "friend." And "philosophy", or φιλοσοφία

means "love of knowledge". So let's say now, "I have a friend."

Ἔχω φίλος.

The next phrase means, "Where does s/he live?"

Ποῦ οἰκεῖ;

One way to remember this is that when someone shouts, "Poo!" you have to ask "Where?" so that you don't step in it. ;) And how would we ask, "Where is the book?"

Ποῦ ἐστιν τὸ βιβλίον;

(Remember, the semi-colon is used for a question mark in Greek.)

The word for "but" or "however" in Ancient Greek is:

ἀλλά

It sounds a little like "alius" in Latin and "else" in English.

Let's try to use this word now. First let's say, "He lives in Greece."

Ἐν τῇ Ἑλλάδι οἰκεῖ.

And let's add now, "But I live in Italy."

Ἀλλά ἐν τῇ Ἰταλίᾳ οἰκῶ.

So altogether it's:

Ἐν τῇ Ἑλλάδι οἰκεῖ, ἀλλά ἐν τῇ Ἰταλίᾳ οἰκῶ.

Let's learn a new word now, which is a little difficult:

βαδίζω

which means, "travel by foot" or usually, "walk"

This ending -ίζω is used to change other words into verbs, so we will see this often. And the rest of the word is:

βαίνω

which we can see is very similar to veniō in Latin, which is in the famous phrase:

Vēnī, vīdī, vīcī.

I came, I saw, I conquered.

Let's use this word now to say, "I walk a lot."

Πολλά βαδίζω.

Remember, the root "poly-" is in the words, "polygamy" and "polytheistic."

And for the story we'll also need the preposition:

πρὸς

When πρὸς is followed by a noun in the accusative form, it means "toward" or "to". This is in the word "prosthesis", literally "add to", but perhaps it's best to think of PROgress, "moving toward" something. Like in the following:

Πρὸς τὸν οἶκον βαδίζω.

I walk to the house.

So to review what was the word meaning, "Where"?

ποῦ

because you have to ask "where" so you don't step on the poo.

And how do we say, "toward" or "to"?

πρὸς

Okay, we're ready to go through this lesson's story now.

Ἔχω φίλος. Ποῦ οἰκεῖ; Ἐν τῇ πόλει οἰκεῖ, ἀλλά ἐν τοῖς ἀγροῖς οἰκῶ. Πρὸς τὸν οἶκον μου βαδίζει. Ἡ οἰκία μικρά ἐστιν, ἀλλά καλή.

Ok, I'm pretty sure you could understand this story and we're well on our way to reading lots of Ancient Greek! But here's a translation into English if there were some parts you didn't catch.

I have a friend. Where does he live? He lives in the city, but I live in the countryside. He walks to my house. The house is small, but beautiful.

APPENDIX

PRONUNCIATION

Ancient Greek pronunciation is different from the modern Greek pronunciation used today. Ancient Greek pronunciation varied across different regions and time periods, but we can make some generalizations based on our understanding of the language.

In ancient times, Greek had a pitch accent, meaning that the pitch of the voice rose or fell on certain syllables in a word. This is different from the stress accent used in modern Greek, where the emphasis is placed on a particular syllable.

Vowels in ancient Greek had long and short versions, with the length of the vowel affecting the rhythm and emphasis of the word. For example, the word ἄνθρωπος (meaning "human being") had a long A sound, whereas the word "ἀγάπη" (meaning "love") had a short A sound.

The first "α" in ἄνθρωπος is long and is pronounced like the "a" in "father." The two "α"s in "ἀγάπη" are short and are pronounced like the "a" in "cat."

Consonants in ancient Greek were pronounced differently than in modern Greek. For example, the letter "beta" was pronounced more like the English "b" sound, whereas in modern Greek it is pronounced more like a "v" sound. The letter "gamma" was pronounced like the "g" in "go" before a vowel, but like the "ng" sound in "sing" before a consonant or at the end of a word.

Overall, Ancient Greek pronunciation is complex and varied, and our understanding of it is based on a combination of historical and linguistic evidence.

It's important to note that the pronunciation of Ancient Greek varied over time and across different regions, and so there was not one uniform pronunciation for each letter. However, based on our understanding of historical and linguistic evidence, here's a general guide to the pronunciation of each letter in Ancient Greek:

Alpha (A, α): pronounced like "ah" as in "father."

Beta (B, β): pronounced like "b" as in "book."

Gamma (Γ, γ): had two different pronunciations. Before a front vowel (like "e" or "i"), it was pronounced like "y" as in "yes." Before a back vowel (like "a," "o," or "u") or a consonant, it was pronounced like "g" as in "go."

Delta (Δ, δ): pronounced like "d" as in "dog."

Epsilon (E, ε): pronounced like "eh" as in "met."

Zeta (Z, ζ): pronounced like "z" as in "zero."

Eta (H, η): pronounced like "ay" as in "day."

Theta (Θ, θ): pronounced like "th" as in "think."

Iota (I, ι): pronounced like "ee" as in "meet."

Kappa (K, κ): pronounced like "k" as in "keep."

Lambda (Λ, λ): pronounced like "l" as in "love."

Mu (M, μ): pronounced like "m" as in "mother."

Nu (N, ν): pronounced like "n" as in "no."

Xi (Ξ, ξ): had a difficult pronunciation that didn't exist in English. It was pronounced like "ks" as in "lacks."

Omicron (O, o): pronounced like "o" as in "boat."

Pi (Π, π): pronounced like "p" as in "pen."

Rho (P, ρ): pronounced like a rolled "r" sound, similar to the Spanish "rr" sound.

Sigma (Σ, σ/ς): pronounced like "s" as in "sea." When at the end of a word, it was written as "ς" (sigma final).

Tau (Τ, τ): pronounced like "t" as in "tall."

Upsilon (Υ, υ): had two different pronunciations. Before a vowel, it was pronounced like "u" as in "use." Before a consonant or at the end of a word, it was pronounced like "ü" as in German "über."

Phi (Φ, φ): pronounced like "f" as in "fish."

Chi (X, χ): pronounced like "ch" as in "loch" (a Scottish word for a lake or a sea inlet).

Psi (Ψ, ψ): had a difficult pronunciation that didn't exist in English. It was pronounced like "ps" as in "lips."

Omega (Ω, ω): pronounced like "o" as in "go."

Again, it's important to keep in mind that this is a general guide, and the pronunciation of each letter may have varied depending on the specific time period and region of Ancient Greece.

KOINE GREEK

Koine Greek is a type of Ancient Greek that was widely spoken from the Hellenistic period (around the 4th century BCE) to the early Byzantine period (around the 7th century CE). Its pronunciation was different from the Classical Greek of earlier times, but it still retained some similarities to the earlier language.

Here's a general guide to the pronunciation of Koine Greek:

Vowels: Koine Greek had both short and long vowels, like Classical Greek. However, the length of the vowel was less important in determining the emphasis of a word. In general, short vowels were pronounced like their modern Greek counterparts (e.g., alpha like "ah," epsilon like "eh"), and long vowels were pronounced for a slightly longer duration (e.g., alpha like "ahh," epsilon like "ehh").

Consonants: The pronunciation of consonants in Koine Greek was generally similar to Classical Greek. However, there were a few notable differences, such as:

The letter "beta" (B, β) was pronounced more like the modern Greek "v" sound, rather than the "b" sound of Classical Greek.

The letter "zeta" (Z, ζ) was pronounced like the modern Greek "z" sound.

The letter "xi" (Ξ, ξ) was pronounced like a combination of "ks" or "x" sound.

The letter "psi" (Ψ, ψ) was pronounced like a combination of "ps" sound.

Accent: In Koine Greek, the pitch accent of earlier periods had disappeared. Instead, the language had a stress accent, with emphasis placed on one syllable of each word.

Overall, the pronunciation of Koine Greek was more similar to the modern Greek pronunciation than the Classical Greek pronunciation. However, it's important to keep in mind that there may have been some variation in the pronunciation of Koine Greek depending on the time period, region, and individual speaker.

FULL STORIES

Πολυμαθῆ νόον ἔχειν οὐ διδάσκει.

Being learned does not make one wise.

Γράμματα μανθάνειν δεῖ καὶ μανθόντα νόον ἔχειν.

One must learn letters, and learning them have reason.

ἐγὼ εἰμὶ παιδίον Ἑλληνικόν, οἰκῶ ἐν ἀγροῖς· ἐν τοῖς ἀγροῖς γεωργός ἐστιν, ὃς γεωργεῖ καὶ ἔχει οἶκον·

I am a Greek child, living in the countryside; in the countryside there is a farmer who farms and has a house;

τέκνον εἰμὶ τοῦ Ἀλεξάνδρου. καὶ ἔχω ἀδελφὸν καὶ ἀδελφήν· τὸ ὄνομα μοι Λεωνίδας ἐστιν. ἐσμὲν οὖν τέκνα τοῦ Ἀλεξάνδρου.

I am a child of Alexander. And I have a brother and a sister; my name is Leonidas. We are then the children of Alexander.

Ἔχομεν οἰκίαν. Ἡ οἰκία καλή ἐστιν. Ἐγγύς ἐστι ποταμός. Ἰχθὺς ἐν τῷ ποτᾰμῷ ἐστιν. Τὸν ἰχθὺν ὁρῶ. Ὁ ἰχθὺς μέγας ἐστίν.

We have a house. The house is beautiful. There is a river nearby. There is a fish in the river. I see the fish. The fish is big.

Ἔχω φίλος. Ποῦ οἰκεῖ; Ἐν τῇ πόλει οἰκεῖ, ἀλλὰ ἐν τοῖς ἀγροῖς οἰκῶ. Πρὸς τὸν οἶκον μου βαδίζει. Ἡ οἰκία μικρά ἐστιν, ἀλλὰ καλή.

I have a friend. Where does he live? He lives in the city, but I live in the countryside. He walks to my house. The house is small, but beautiful.

Printed in Great Britain
by Amazon

40745903R00037